street football

Paul Mason
and Sarah Eason

cover stories

First published in 2011 by Wayland

Copyright © Wayland 2011

Wayland
Hachette Children's Books
338 Euston Road
London NW1 3BH

Wayland Australia
Level 17/207 Kent Street
Sydney NSW 2000

Concept by Joyce Bentley

Commissioned by Debbie Foy and
Rasha Elsaeed

Produced for Wayland by Calcium
Designer: Paul Myerscough
Editor: Sarah Eason

Photographer: Adam Lawrence

British Library Cataloguing in Publication Data

Mason, Paul, 1967–
    Street football.
    1. Soccer—Juvenile literature.
    2. Street life—Juvenile literature.
    I. Title II. Eason, Sarah.
    796.3'34-dc22

ISBN: 978 0 7502 6460 0

Printed in China

Wayland is a division of Hachette Children's
Books, an Hachette UK company.

www.hachette.co.uk

Acknowledgements:

International Street Soccer Association
2–3, 28b; Nelson de Kok/Ruud Bos 24;
Rex Features: Canadian Press 16–17;
Shutterstock: Aniad 25, Alex Jackson 1,
Jan Kranendonk 2r, 2t, 7, 30–31,
Magicinfoto 4–5; Kim Tamburri 13.

thepeople

themoves

thetalk

STREET FOOTBALL

Street football is fast, fierce, creative and groundbreaking. It is a style of football that has come from the 'street' – where players perform stunning acrobatic moves with the ball to outwit an opponent.

WHAT'S DIFFERENT?

Street football is all about using creative moves to control a ball within a street football game. Unlike association football, which has just one game and one set of rules, street football has lots of games and each has its own rules or scoring system. Street footballers attempt to outplay their opponents with fresh, creative, jaw-dropping moves. Many of the skills performed by street footballers would not be allowed in an association football game.

FROM THE STREET

Street football moves began on the streets of Amsterdam. These players broke away from traditional football and started to invent their own new and creative style of football. The young footballers played on the streets, juggling the ball in new and inventive ways – often never seen before. Their impressive moves caught on throughout the Netherlands, and are now spreading right across the world.

Type 'street football' into www.youtube.com to see what this amazing sport is all about!

What is freestyle football?

Street footballers perfect their control of the ball by juggling it with their body, arms, legs, feet and even their heads. This is called freestyle football.

Street footballers practise freestyle moves to improve both their control of the ball and the moves they use within a street football game.

THE BEAUTIFUL GAME

If you want to play a fresh and fun ball sport, play street football! Catch on to the latest street moves and the most inventive ways to out-manoeuvre your opponent. Here are just some of the reasons to play this cool, street smart sport:

1 You don't need to belong to a club or team to play street football. As long as you have trainers, a ball and some space to kick around, you can play street football.

2 Street football helps you to develop amazing ball control, which you can use in street football games or association football matches. Good ball control skills will improve your game in any footballing situation.

3 If you don't like lots of rules, try street football. There are fewer regulations than in association football, because street football encourages individual style and focuses on *your* abilities and talents. You don't have to fit in with a set way of playing football – instead you can work on developing your own creative skills and style.

4 If you become really good at street football and come up with an amazing move, it could even be named after you! Most of the great street footballers have invented moves that now carry their name. The 'de Ruud' move is named after Ruud Bos and street football legend Issy 'Hitman' Hamdaoui created the 'Issy Akka'. Having a football move named after you is the ultimate street football mark of respect.

5 Street football is more than just a way of playing football – these days it's a whole culture. Street footballers call their culture stilo, meaning style. You can tap into street football music, language and even street football clothing.

Street football is clever, creative, dynamic and street smart. It's football with an inbuilt 'wow factor'. Who wouldn't want to play it?

THE MOVES

The exciting moves performed by street footballers aren't just designed to impress a crowd. They are used to outwit an opponent in a street game. To street footballers the moves shown here are 'basic' – to most people they are highly impressive!

AKKA

The footballer rolls the foot over the ball, moving it from side to side. This confuses the opponent into believing the ball will move in a certain direction so the footballer can move it in the opposite direction and out of reach.

THE FLICK

The footballer flicks the ball up and to the opponent's side. He then kicks the ball behind the opponent and runs past to collect it.

KNEE AKKA

In this move, the ball is flicked off the ground with the footballer's foot then hit with the outside of the knee. The footballer uses their foot to flick the ball away from the opponent.

AKKA 3000

This is another move used to keep control of the ball. The footballer flicks the ball up to waist height and spins 180 degrees to face the opponent. He then uses a knee akka to flick the ball away from the opponent.

akka

the flick

akka 3000

knee akka

THE AKKA

Use the akka to outwit the opponent and to keep control of the ball.

You will need:

- football
- trainers
- space to practise

1

Start about a metre away from your opponent. This will give you enough room to perform the move.

2

Move the ball to one side with the outside part of the foot.

3 Push the ball far in the opposite direction with the inside of the same foot.

4 Just before losing control of the ball, use the other foot to bring the ball back towards you and past the opponent.

Got it?

As the opponent moves in the 'fake' direction of the ball, you can quickly move the ball away from them and out of reach!

Type 'street football akka' into www.youtube.com to see how this is done!

11

LIVE FOR FOOTBALL

CHRISTINE TAMBURRI'S STORY

About two years ago, I was beginning to find 'normal' football really boring. The coaches were always shouting at us and everyone had to play the same way. Even though I really loved football, it felt like all the fun was being sucked out of it.

Then I started playing street football. It was completely different – my coach encouraged me to try out brand new techniques and skills, and to play football the way *I* wanted to. Eventually my skills improved and when I got to use them in matches, it only made me want to practise more!

After that I started searching the internet for new moves. I practised street moves all the time and I kept on looking for new ways to improve my game. I didn't do it to win medals or trophies – I did it just because I loved the game.

Learning complex moves like the akka 3000 was a real breakthrough for me and a major achievement. Street football has given me a boatload of satisfaction, and I've got a *lot* of respect from my friends, too. These days, I don't just play street soccer – I live it!

AKKA 3000

You can use the akka 3000 for passing and shooting, or getting past an opponent.

You will need:

- **football** • **trainers**
- **space to practise**

1 Set up so that the opponent is to the right of you.

2 Use the foot to flick the ball up into the air, to waist height.

3 Swivel around in a full circle as the ball rises up in the air.

4

Bring the leg up in a similar fashion to the knee akka (page 8) as you turn. Tap the ball with the knee, up into the air and away from the opponent.

Type 'street football akka 3000' into www.youtube.com to see this great move!

5

Use the foot to kick the ball around the opponent.

Got it?

The opponent will move after the ball as you perform the first three steps of the move. The twist in step 4 allows you to then swivel away from the opponent and move the ball in another direction!

CRISTIANO RONALDO

THE STATS

Name: Cristiano Ronaldo
Born: 5 February 1985
Place of birth: Madeira
Nationality: Portuguese
Job: Professional footballer

GROWING UP

Cristiano grew up on the small island of Madeira. He started playing football on the island's dusty back streets and quickly grew into a brilliant performer. By the time he was 12 years old, Cristiano was the best footballer on the island.

ON THE STREET

Cristiano perfected his awesome football skills on the streets of Madeira, and claims that the best – and most creative – footballers come from the street. He regularly showcases his stunning street style on the professional pitch, showing off street football moves or impressive freestyle juggling skills.

FROM STREET TO STAR

In 2009, Cristiano was named FIFA World Player of the Year. In the same year, Manchester United sold him to football club Real Madrid for an incredible £80 million! Cristiano is currently the most expensive and most highly paid professional footballer in the world.

SPOTTED!

Cristiano began to play for Sporting Clube du Portugal. His exceptional skills were quickly spotted by leading clubs, such as Liverpool and Juventus, but it was Manchester United who bought the player when he was just 18 years old – for a staggering £12 million! It was the biggest amount of money ever paid by a club for a teenage footballer.

DARREN LAVER

Street football coach Darren Laver is passionate about his game and teaches it all over the world. Radar thinks there's nothing Darren doesn't know about street football – so we put him to the test...

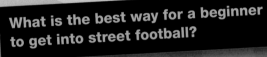

What is the best way for a beginner to get into street football?

The best way is to find a coach who can teach you core street football skills. Check out Fan Club (page 32) to find out how to get a street football coach into your school!

What equipment do you need to play street football?

That's the great thing about street football – all you need is a pair of trainers and a ball. Almost anything can be used as goal markers – bags and jumpers are the most popular. That's the beauty of the sport, you can set up and just play almost anywhere!

Where can you play street football?

You don't need a regular pitch to play street football. All you need is some space, such as a park or a yard. As long as your environment is spacious and safe, you can play street football there.

Is street football more dangerous than association football?

Street football is probably less dangerous. In street football you play creatively to outwit your opponent. Association football focuses more on aggressive tackling, in which players are more likely to be injured.

Can you use street skills in association or professional football?

Not all street football moves can be used in association football, but moves such as the akka and the flick are used by players like Ronaldinho and Ronaldo all the time in professional games.

Do you use stilo in street football coaching sessions?

I play street football music during our coaching sessions. Using stilo music is a brilliant way to pump up the creative atmosphere in a session – it gets players into the zone and really improves their creativity and skills with the ball.

STREET SPEAK

Get your stilo up to speed with this easy street speak guide.

klapper
to make the ball move very quickly just by using the soles of the feet

panna
placing the ball between your opponent's legs (also known as a nutmeg)

search
to move the ball so that the opponent is forced to turn in a full circle

send
to use a trick move to send your opponent in the wrong direction

annap
'panna' spelt backwards. In this move the player places the ball between the opponent's legs, but from *behind* the opponent – so the move is a 'backwards' panna

shock
to make the opponent flinch by pretending to kick the ball towards them

stilo
the word street footballers use to describe their culture

drag
to slide the ball backwards and forwards in front of your opponent so that they are thrown off balance

vanish
to make the ball disappear from the opponent's sight, such as by rolling the ball behind you or even hiding it inside your shirt!

GLOSSARY

aggressive
fierce or rough

animated
made into a moving picture

forfeit
to do something as a 'punishment', or to give something up

groundbreaking
new and never seen before

immortalised
when someone is changed in some way so that they will 'live' forever or is likely to be famous for a long time

orbit
to make a complete circle around something

out-manoeuvre
to move more efficiently than someone else. If you out-manoeuvre an opponent in street football, you move the ball away from them and out of their reach

outwit
to be better than an opponent

promo (promotional event)
a gathering in which something is brought to the attention of many people

rotation
a circular movement

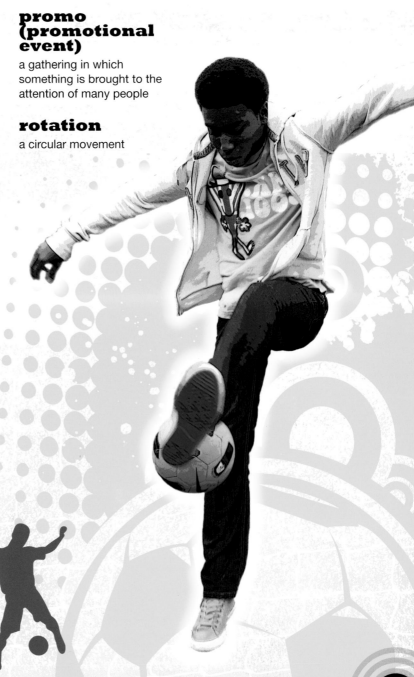

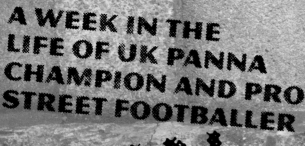

A WEEK IN THE LIFE OF UK PANNA CHAMPION AND PRO STREET FOOTBALLER

SEAN THOMPSON

blog   news   events

SUNDAY

I was so tired this morning! I was up really early yesterday to go to a street football promo event. We were really on form and did loads of freestyle moves. The crowd went mad!

MONDAY

I watched a bit of *Rule the Street* (a street soccer DVD) for some inspiration, then went to the local park for a bit of freestyle juggling. I'm always trying to come up with new tricks and I think I have a few in the making.

TUESDAY

I rolled out of bed at about 7.30am, had a quick shower and got dressed before my boss picked me up. At work I managed to pin down a booking for a street football

blog   **news**   **events**

show at an upcoming Adidas promo event. When I got home I put on some Eminem and did some akkas and head balances to get ready for the event.

WEDNESDAY

We taught at an after-school club today, helping the kids work on basic akkas. Some of them are doing really well. After a bit of a warm-up we played life in a bottle (page 31), a cool game where players aim to knock over bottles filled with water.

THURSDAY

Today we headed to the Adidas event. I spent the morning setting up the stage, then I had some time to kill, so I practised my soles of the feet (page 29) and akka 3000 (page 14). I practise whenever I can.

FRIDAY

I had a busy day at work today preparing for tomorrow's show at Manchester United. We have been asked to do a freestyle show at a club event. Lots of the top players are going to be there – so it's more important than ever that we're on top form.

SATURDAY

I spent the morning at Manchester United football ground making sure the music, lighting and stage for the show tonight would all be OK. The show was brilliant – and nobody made any mistakes. Result!

23

NELSON & RUUD

THE GAME BOYS

Nelson de Kok

Ruud Bos

THE STATS

Name: Nelson de Kok
Born: 22 August 1986
Place of birth: Goirle, the Netherlands
Job: Professional street footballer

THE STATS

Name: Ruud Bos
Born: 14 May 1983
Place of birth: Oss, the Netherlands
Job: Professional street footballer

NELSON FINDS FREESTYLE

As a child, Nelson lived, breathed and slept football. As a teenager he discovered freestyle football – and never looked back. Nelson's freestyle skills were exceptional and in 2003 he wowed crowds with his impressive moves at the Masters of the Game freestyle football championships in Amsterdam. Almost as impressive as his freestyle moves was Nelson's age – he was just 17 years old and one of the youngest players to ever take part in the competition.

RUUD AND STREET

Ruud started playing football when he was just five years old. As he grew up, he became more and more interested in mastering complex football moves. His stunning freestyle skills marked him out as an outstanding player and shortly after appearing in the Masters of the Game tournament in Amsterdam, he was invited to work alongside Nelson on the *FIFA Street* game.

GAMEBOY HEROES

In 2004, the two players starred together in the computer game *FIFA Street*. The game immortalised the footballers as true street football superheroes. The electrifying animated duo performed outstanding street football moves on screen, making the game a massive international success. It also catapulted the two young sportsmen into street football stardom.

RULING THE STREET

In 2006, Nelson and Ruud followed their success in *FIFA Street* with two DVDs, *Rule of the Street* and *Soccer King*. *Soccer King* is a 'how to' DVD in which the street football super-team teach cutting-edge stunts and moves. *Rule of the Street* showcases the footballers' street and freestyle football skills. It has become the ultimate must-see film for fans and players everywhere.

TOP OF THEIR GAME

Today, Nelson and Ruud are recognised as two of the world's hottest street football stars. They regularly showcase street football moves on TV, support workshops for young up-and-coming street footballers and are in demand from leading sports companies for their advertising power. When it comes to football, Nelson and Ruud rule!

Type 'Nelson de Kok street football' into www.youtube.com to watch him in action!

SPIN THE WORLD

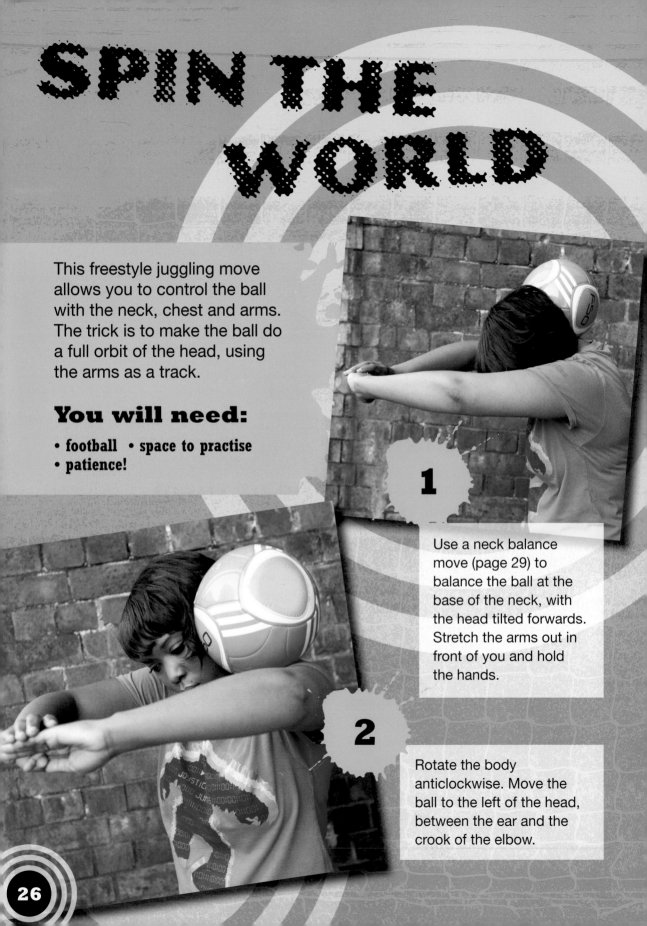

This freestyle juggling move allows you to control the ball with the neck, chest and arms. The trick is to make the ball do a full orbit of the head, using the arms as a track.

You will need:

- **football** • **space to practise**
- **patience!**

1

Use a neck balance move (page 29) to balance the ball at the base of the neck, with the head tilted forwards. Stretch the arms out in front of you and hold the hands.

2

Rotate the body anticlockwise. Move the ball to the left of the head, between the ear and the crook of the elbow.

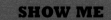

Keep turning the body so that the ball moves to the front of the head. It should rest between the hands and head.

3

4

Continue to turn anticlockwise until the ball reaches a point between the right ear and right elbow. Then let it return to its starting place at the back of the head.

Got it?

The ball should have made one full rotation around the head. Keep practising the move until you can send the ball around the head twice – without stopping!

FREESTYLE MOVES

neck balance

soles of the feet

Freestyle moves are used by street footballers to improve their ball control skills. If a player can control the ball, they can control the game – and win!

HEAD BALANCE

The footballer throws the ball onto the forehead while leaning back. They move the feet from side to side to help balance the ball.

NECK BALANCE

The ball is thrown up gently. As it comes down, the footballer moves the head down and forwards, and cushions the ball on the back of the neck. They may bring the arms out to the side to stop the ball from rolling off.

SPIN THE WORLD

The footballer goes into a neck balance, then brings the arms forwards and hands together. The footballer nudges the ball to one side and spins it towards the arms. The ball is rotated around the arms and back to the neck.

SOLES OF THE FEET

The footballer lies on their back and throws the ball up above the chest. They bring up one foot and balance the ball on the sole. Then the footballer puts both legs in the air and juggles the ball between the feet.

spin the world

Type 'street football freestyle tricks' into www.youtube.com to see more juggling moves.

head balance

THE GAMES

Street football games are exciting, fast-paced displays of freestyle magic. Unlike association football, street football games can be played with a handful of players (some with just two). There are many street football games, but here are some of the best.

1. 3 V 3 SWITCH

Six footballers play, with three players in each team (3 v 3). The size and type of ball used to play the game is changed (or switched) every minute. Lots of different balls are used, from tennis balls and footballs to American footballs. The aim is for players to score as many goals as they can in two minutes. Game on!

2. 3 V 3 MINES

Six players play this game with three players in each team. Two balls are used. One ball is the mine and is placed on a cone in the middle of the playing area. The other ball is the football. Players aim to score as many goals in the opposition's net as they can, without knocking the mine off the cone as they play. If a player does knock off the mine, their team must do a forfeit – chosen by the other team!

3. 1 V 1 PANNA

Panna is the Dutch word for 'nutmeg' (the football term for playing the ball through your opponent's legs). There are two players in this game. Each tries to 'out-panna' the other player. The player who scores the most pannas in two minutes wins.

4. 3 V 3 PANNA FREEZE

In Panna Freeze six footballers play, with three players on each team. The aim is to score as many goals against the opposition as possible. The twist is that if a player is 'panna-ed' (an opponent kicks the ball through their legs), they must freeze for 20 seconds before continuing to play!

5. LIFE IN A BOTTLE

This is a game in which, instead of goals, each team has two open plastic bottles filled with water. Six footballers play, with three in each team. Players aim the ball at the other team's bottle. The aim is to knock over the opponent's bottle, so spilling the water inside. The defender has to quickly pick up the bottle, to avoid losing water. After three minutes, the team with the most water in their bottle wins.

People to talk to

Want to be part of one of the coolest sports on the streets? Then get into street football! There are lots of organisations that can help you kick off your game.

International Street Soccer Association (ISSA)
ISSA run street football training courses across the UK and USA and coach the latest moves. Darren Laver, Radar consultant, heads all ISSA courses. So if you want to get street football into your school, go to:
www.internationalstreetsoccer.com

Free speech

Chat online to other freestyle football fans at:
www.beyondfootball.com

DVDs & APPs

Check out the *ISSA Ball Fusion* DVD and find out all there is to know about street football. Prepare to be amazed and inspired! You can also download the ISSA street football app *Street Skills*.

Watch *Billy Wingrove's Learn Freestyle Football* DVD and pick up tips from this expert freestyle footballer. Find the DVD at:
www.billywingrove.com

INDEX

your mission:
To seek out more
cool Radar reads...

radar

978 0 7502 6442 6

978 0 7502 6455 6

978 0 7502 6456 3

978 0 7502 6454 9

978 0 7502 6441 9

More Radar titles coming soon!

Graffiti Culture
Street Art
Cool Brands
Body Decoration

The Armed Services
The Special Forces
Undercover Operations
Police Forensics

Being a Pro Footballer
Being a DJ
Being a Stuntman
Being a Snowboarder
Being a Model
Being a Formula 1 Racing Driver
Celebrity Make-up Artist
Celebrity Fashion Stylist
Celebrity Photographer

Are you on the Radar?